Mastering the Basics of Selling

Orville H. (Pete) Casto, Jr.

authorHOUSE®

AuthorHouse™
1663 Liberty Drive
Bloomington, IN 47403
www.authorhouse.com
Phone: 1-800-839-8640

First published by AuthorHouse 6/22/2010

ISBN: 978-1-4490-4074-1 (e)
ISBN: 978-1-4490-4072-7 (sc)
ISBN: 978-1-4490-4073-4 (hc)

Library of Congress Control Number: 2010907658

Printed in the United States of America
Bloomington, Indiana

This book is printed on acid-free paper.

Dedication

I dedicate this book and all its proceeds to my four children: Gregory Alan, Julianne Elizabeth, Jennifer Lynn, Jocelyn Leigh and my ten grand-children. It is my wish that the proceeds be used for their educational expenses.

Father

Orville H. (Pete) Casto, Jr.

And

I wish to thank my wife (Diane) for her encouragement to write this book.

Husband

Table of Contents

Foreword

It is often said of someone who has great expertise in his field, "He wrote the book." In *Mastering the Basics of Selling*, Pete Casto *has written* the book. Pete goes to the very bedrock principles of sales success, principles which he practiced without fail over his long and highly successful career.

I can think of no one better qualified to speak to the fundamentals of selling than Pete. I had the privilege, as Business Director of Europe and the Americas for a major business unit at Union Carbide Corporation, of working closely with Pete for over ten years. I saw him in action, selling hundreds of millions of dollars of some of the company's key products to some of our most important customers. These companies were leaders in their industries, with enormous purchasing power. Our products were strategic for them; these were high-profile purchases. Pete's focus and tenacity were legendary, both within our company and with his customers. I once had the V.P. of Purchasing at a major account call me and say, "I'll sign the contract on one condition: you have to promise that Pete will not call me for a month. I need a rest." This contract was worth more than $100 million.

Pete was the master of in-depth selling, cultivating contacts at every level, from the V.P. of Purchasing right down to the shipping dock of a client company. No competitor had a chance once Pete had our company entrenched, and as junior-level people in our client companies rose to become the V.P. of Purchasing—or even the CEO in some cases—this became even more true.

Pete was also the master of the sales interface: representing both the company to the customer and the customer to the company. In short, Pete Casto was the master, no matter how complex the situation, of applying the basic principles in this book, every day, to achieve a successful result.

Everyone in sales or sales management, whether they are just beginning their career in sales or are already well established should read this book.

Dr. Rick Jones, Principal Dauntless Chemical LLC
Ridgefield, CT

Preface

WRITING THIS BOOK HAS BROUGHT back many memories of the people who impacted my life. I would be remiss to not acknowledge my parents foremost; their frequent encouragements and the examples of hard work they demonstrated influenced me throughout my childhood. They are both deceased now, but not before they enjoyed seeing me achieve several of my accomplishments and awards.

Today, I have what I expect they did: much enjoyment in watching my four children (Gregory, Julianne, Jennifer and Jocelyn) accomplish many successes in their careers. I recall once having a conversation with my son about slowing down, and he remarked, "Dad, you're not a good example to be giving that kind of advice."

Later, I was praising my youngest daughter on the way she handled the details of purchasing her first new home, and her response was, "Dad, I observed and learned from the best." As the old saying goes, the apples do not fall far from the tree.

Not only did the events throughout my early childhood help shape my life, they enabled me to form many of the strengths and abilities that guided me toward a professional selling career. Yes, I went through several fields that I would like to have "become" when I grew up, from a football or basketball coach, to a train engineer and a physical therapist.

However, as you read about my early life, you can readily see the career I was heading toward. I went into professional sales, and was it a beautiful ride! I have no regrets!

I was born into a loving, hard-working family in central West Virginia on June 17, 1937. My father and mother went through the eighth and sixth grades, respectively. Following the death of his own father, my father dropped out of school and worked at odd jobs to support himself. As for my mother, she was at the tender age of five when her own mother died. She made it through the sixth grade, which was the highest grade level available in that little country school. My mother liked school so much that she studied the sixth grade materials for two additional years. The next school she would have gone to was six or seven miles away over a wooded, country dirt road. There was no available transportation, which effectively ended her formal education.

From the time I was old enough to remember, my parents encouraged us children to get an education. To make ends meet, they both worked at odd jobs to provide shelter, food, and clothing. Following their advice at a young age, I likewise started dividing my time between school, sports, and working at odd jobs.

My summer jobs started with cutting lawns, earning $3.00 to $4.00 a day, and working on a nearby farm, where I milked seven to eight cows mornings and evenings. I also raised turkeys to sell during the Thanksgiving period. During the Christmas season, I would walk miles through the woods, searching for Christmas trees I could sell to the local residents.

I went through my first five years of elementary schooling in a small, single-classroom school where one teacher (Mrs. Summers) taught all five grades. When it became time to move into the sixth grade, this meant going to the nearby town where there was a large, two-floor brick school. Yes, I was scared, but I survived, and for the seventh grade, I moved to a yet larger school that covered the seventh through the twelfth grades.

From that point onward, life changed quickly for me. I resumed working every day at the nearby farm, milking seven to eight cows mornings and evenings. I had learned at an early age to manage my time. I would start around 5:00 a.m., get back home at 6:45 a.m., clean up and run a mile to school so I could practice junior-high basketball. I would shower and be ready for the classes that ran from 9:00 a.m. to 3:00 p.m. I loved football, but beyond the seventh grade, I was much too small to play. Yet, I loved the sport so much that I talked my way into becoming a manager for the team. There again, the football practice was from 3:30 p.m. through 5:30 p.m. As I struggled to meet all these schedules, I learned a good lesson on how to plan and organize my time so I could also keep my job at the farm. Because working there on Friday evenings would prevent me from being involved with the football team, I worked out an arrangement with the owner.

Planning and organizing my day was critical. Yet, at that time, little did I understand that all of these skills were setting the stage for the key role they would play in my professional sales career. Throughout my younger years, I had learned from my mother and father that when you make commitments, such as cutting the lawn, milking the cows, and promising some family that you would locate a Christmas tree for them, you kept your word.

As I think back to the key events that helped form my selling strengths and abilities, I recall a couple of incidents. In high school, the tenth-grade English class was responsible for publishing the school newspaper, *The Cardinal*, which happened to be having money problems. I volunteered to sell ads. I was so successful that the English teacher, Mrs. White, requested that I slow down, because the volume of new ads was causing the advertising pages to outweigh the articles.

The second incident also occurred while I was in high school. At the time, the Curtis Publishing Company launched a magazine sales contest, offering the school a percentage on the volume of sales. I won the contest and was recognized at the year-end Awards Assembly. These activities taught me how to utilize the basic selling skills that I would later use throughout my career.

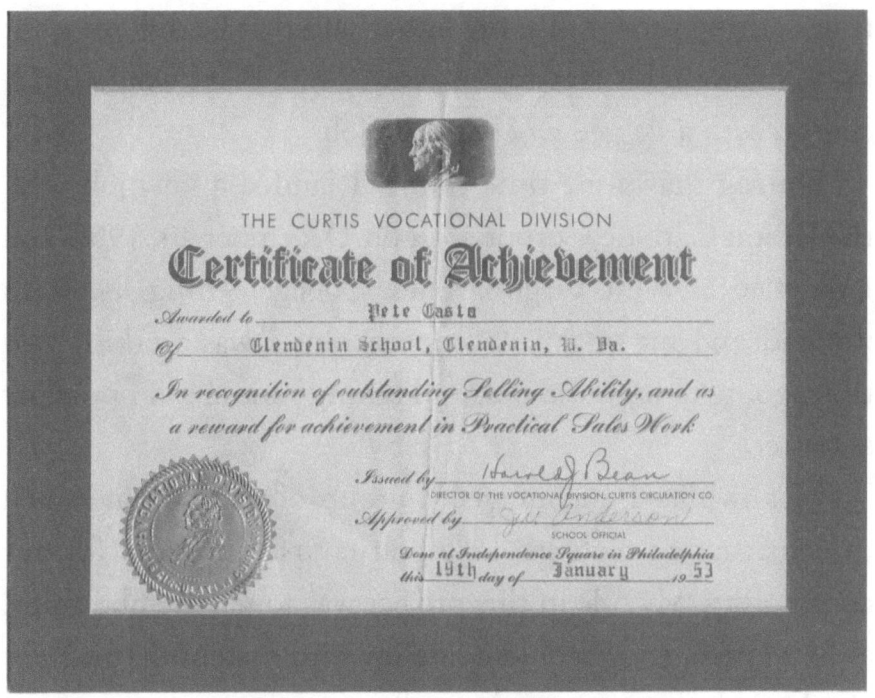

THE CURTIS VOCATIONAL DIVISION

Certificate of Achievement

Awarded to _____ Pete Casto _____

Of _____ Clendenin School, Clendenin, W. Va. _____

In recognition of outstanding Selling Ability, and as a reward for achievement in Practical Sales Work

Issued by _____ Harold J Bean _____
DIRECTOR OF THE VOCATIONAL DIVISION, CURTIS CIRCULATION CO.

Approved by _____ J. H. Anderson _____
SCHOOL OFFICIAL

Done at Independence Square in Philadelphia
this 19th day of January 19 53

When I graduated from high school, there were no expectations that I would go to college. In other words, I was from the other side of the tracks, and it was clear that money would be a major problem. However, in spite of that, my parents encouraged me to pursue a higher education.

I worked during the summer leading up to my enrollment at Glenville State College and completed my freshman year. The following summer, I landed a job at an oil and gasoline producing company. Immediately afterwards, I purchased my first car. My father was concerned that the expenses of owning a car, added to the cost of attending college, would cause me to drop out of school. We had some direct conversations until I assured him that I would enroll in night school at West Virginia State College and complete my education. Several times during those talks, my father said that he did not want me to follow in his footsteps. I assured him that I would finish college with a degree *and* keep the job.

During that same time frame, I landed a new job with the Union Carbide Corporation on December 10, 1957, and I enrolled at West Virginia State College. Things between my dad and me began to smooth out; I was working full time, going to night school, and taking nine credit hours per semester.

Meanwhile, I encouraged a group of local businessmen to construct an eighteen-hole golf course and pool for our community. My role in this project was to sell memberships, at $300 each, so we could come up with matching funds for our loan. I was successful at selling over 80 percent of the memberships, and we built that eighteen-hole course.

Management at Union Carbide began to notice that if I could work eight hours, go to school three to four nights a week, and on the week-ends, sell a golf course concept, then my name should be placed up for interviews with their sales organization. I was soon offered a sales position in the General Sales Force, working out of the Atlanta, Georgia, sales office and calling on accounts located in Alabama, Georgia, Florida, and parts of South Carolina. Again, I began to put to work the values I had learned early in life, applying them to my sales assignments. I quickly started setting huge sales records, which earned me several promotions and salary increases.

Looking back on those forty-four years, I realize I was blessed with exceptionally good health, missing only one week with the flu. I worked with Excellent Management/ Marketing, Product Management, /R&D Personnel and Customer Service. Today I live comfortably and enjoy seeing my children succeed in their chosen professions. They have given me ten very beautiful grandchildren.

In reflecting back over my origins and the events that shaped my life, I realized that if I could accomplish the levels of success I achieved, then the majority of the readers of this book could achieve similar results by following specific concepts. That's when the idea of this book took root: why not write a book that would outline the selling concepts I've applied through the years, breaking them down to their simplest form?

Using state highway maps on each of the states of my sales responsibilities, I would plot my days based on where my customers were located. I would study the driving times between each account, and outline the best routes that would allow me to save time, while maximizing the number of calls I could make in a day's time. Implementing this strategy was very effective for me, and it's something that you, too, can try. You want your coverage to be cost effective. Once you have completed this exercise, you could then organize your customers in groups, labeling them Group A," "Group B," etc. You'll also need to establish how frequently to call them: every thirty, forty-five, or sixty days. This will take time. However, as I look back on my own experience, this was one of the smartest exercises I went through.

Then, as I worked with each major account, I addressed each of the following topics:

I) *Planning and organizing your territory and your accounts.* Where are they located? What are the travel times between each of them? This will help you in budgeting your time and monies in a most productive manner.

II) *Establishing your objectives and strategies for each account and sales territory.* Know what it will take to achieve the objectives. This will also allow you to better understand each of the business area's objectives, while effectively preparing you for each and every call. Review key issues that you want to cover on each call, and decide with whom you want to address them.

III) *Know Your Products* and how they are produced, while understanding how they are used by your customers. Are these products a major part of the success of your company? In other words, would they be easy to eliminate from production? Look for the positive benefit areas to tie your products into your customer, i.e., raw material strengths, freight costs, and warehouse locations versus customer locations, etc. Also, keep a folder in which you file a copy of product specifications on all your major products. Carry the folder with you at all times.

IV)   *Know Your Competition* as thoroughly as you know your own company. This is a strategy that pays off on every arena, even in sports. As the salesman on the account, you are the quarterback. When contract negotiations begin, you must know your strengths versus those of your competition. Have the details handy, and help lead your management team in making a successful proposal.

V) *Know Your Customers.* This is most critical in understanding as much data as you possible can. First, who are the decision makers? How critical is the product to your customer's business? What are the relationships between your competition and your customers? Are there any special pricing arrangements from past dealings, terms, etc.? Are there inventory floor-stock, price-protection clauses that you should be aware of? Are there any special R&D programs that would give you or your competition an advantage? Know where your customers are going in the marketplace and who they are competing against.

VI) *Don't Promise More Than You Can Deliver.* Be truthful and dependable at all times. Your credibility will follow you throughout your career, no matter what position you hold.

VII) *Communicate in a Timely Manner.* Competitive activities, problems, and opportunities should be well documented, followed with your recommendations.

Utilize all methods of communications: report of calls, e-mails, faxes and for situations that require quick actions, use the telephone.

VIII) *Sell in-depth.* Use your company's personnel and internal resources at the proper time. Expose the benefits of doing business with you and your company.

IX) *Keep a positive attitude and show enthusiasm.* Handle the details in a timely manner; don't put them off for your customer service representative (or others) to communicate. Take every opportunity to make that direct follow-up with your customer.

X) *Show Respect to Your customers.* Call for appointments. If for any reason, you will be unable to keep your appointment, be sure to telephone with details.

Three basic areas that will help you keep everyone within your company informed on each of your customers are as follows:

- Know where you have been with this customer.

- Know where you are currently with this customer.

- Know where you are planning to go with this customer.

This is nothing more than a one-page snapshot of each

client's history that you, as the salesman, can put together for your management to review.

XI)   *Account Profile Planning Sheets.* This is another critical area that you will want to go through in gathering data on your accounts. See Appendix section for details.

You will find yourself using this data on a daily basis. Once the data is compiled it will give you a play book on your customers. These documents will be very useful during joint calls with your management and when it comes to educating new personnel coming into your business area.

~ Chapter 1 ~

Plan and Organize Your Approach

SELLING IS AN ACTIVITY THAT can be done by one person, or by a team of two or more salespeople. It is a lot like any other profession; you have to like and enjoy the field you work within to be successful. How you approach it makes all the difference to your success levels. Selling can truly be very *rewarding*.

Whether you have just started your career in sales or have been in the profession for a number of years, or if you're making a major career change altogether, you will need a sound understanding of the "basics of selling skills." This will give you a better understanding of the keys to success as you focus on the sales opportunities at hand.

First, let's do a self-examination. Are you ready to make a total commitment to an age-old profession? And if you are, let's start by answering the following key questions:

1. Do you like the sounds of a selling profession?
2. Do you believe in yourself? Are you a self-starter who is self-motivated? Are you ready to start new projects right away, or are you a procrastinator?
3. Do you believe in the company and the products you're representing?

4. Do you have the personal integrity that will help build credibility with your clients?

5. Is your vision for achieving success strong enough to allow you to establish goals and objectives, and to pursue those goals until they're accomplished?

6. Are you undaunted at the prospect of working the hours that it takes to succeed?

7. Do you have the stomach to take the hard knocks, to pick yourself up, to not take rejections personally but go right back to selling again?

8. Are you flexible? Even though your competition may beat you out, can you keep your eyes on the goal and go back with another game plan to bring your client company's management back to the table? In other words, at the end of the day, do you know that you did not give up?

9. When you look in the mirror at the close of each day, can you truly feel good about what you see and feel?

If you can answer yes to 90 percent of these questions, then you can feel confident that you're headed toward becoming a successful salesperson.

Once you've conducted this self-evaluation, your next step is to plan and organize your sales territory. This will be the first of several key steps that will help you analyze the accounts in your geographical jurisdiction. The goal of this analysis is to obtain a solid grasp of your customers' location, the products they produce, their size, and their potential importance to your company. Based on this analysis, you can classify your accounts into categories, such as A, B, and C.

This process will develop into several discussions with your manager. You will begin to gain insight into the direction of your customers' thought patterns and priorities. This will also give you a stronger understanding of the products and their importance to each of your customers, and to the company you represent. In the area of planning, you will want to understand where your competitors stack up against your company. Learning their strengths and weaknesses will help you plan an effective sales pitch. In-depth market knowledge will also enhance your understanding of your clients' statements during your sales call. Your own knowledge of the market will allow you to feed accurate intelligence and data back to your management.

Let's start organizing and identifying your customers. First, you will want to interview your customer service personnel. They can be an excellent starting point for information on existing sales records, and can answer questions, such as: Which products are selling? Who is calling in the orders? How regularly are they paying their accounts?

You may be able to retrieve existing client records that go back several years, and may even find sales personnel who are still working for the company and who can provide you with customer information on some of your accounts. It does not hurt to question all parties and gain as much intelligence as possible.

Another source of information is manufacturing directories that states often publish. These directories provide a listing of companies, their manufacturing location, the number of employees on their staff, and where their headquarters are located.

When you come across a new account and you have no previous sales records for that account, the first thing you will want to do is establish a file on what products they're buying and from whom. Getting a new account to approve your product is a time-consuming process. You may decide to request assistance from your research and development or technical personnel, to help you become acquainted with the customer's technical personnel. This will facilitate obtaining the approvals you will need to process a sale. If you obtain these approvals up front, prior to receiving an actual order, this will expedite delivery when the order does come through. Prior approvals also prevent potential delays, and a delayed order may cause you to start off on the wrong foot with your new customer..

The first specific step to getting your product approved is to work through your client's purchasing department to obtain a copy of their specifications. Have them tell you who you should contact in their technical department. This will give you the names of others with whom you can develop future contact.

This process is called in-depth selling, and it is often the way to start proceeding when you locate a new customer. Know your own strengths and weaknesses. Build on your strengths, and work to improve your weaknesses, Be honest with your customer. Keep a smile on your face, consider and show enthusiasm to the wildest of ideas, and examine them closely before you close the door. And think positive. A salesperson without a positive attitude would be likened to a "cowboy" without a horse. Everyone is different, but when you are in the sales profession, you must find the proverbial silver lining within yourself, even in the darkest of defeats. An example of a defeat can be the loss of an order. Examine the reasons that caused that particular defeat, learn from it, and become a better salesperson.

SCORE

UNION
CARBIDE
CORPORATION
Chemicals & Plastics

U.S. Area
Refrigerant Sales Force

O. H. CASTO, JR.

Percentage Increase
Second Half 1971

~ *Chapter 2* ~

Establishing Objectives

ESTABLISHING OBJECTIVES AND STRATEGIES WILL take time. The longer you maintain your sales coverage of an account, the more these objectives will change from year to year. You will need to clarify the objectives and strategies you plan to accomplish in the short and long term.

As you approach a customer, your first pass may be as simple as getting to know the leaders and the different functions within the account. The second objective would concentrate on the products they produce, and on those products they would potentially buy from your company. At that point, you can project the sales units you propose to go after. Your objectives for the first year could look something like the following:

- Who are the key decision makers within the new account? What position do they hold? Get to know the players.

- What products do they produce, and in which quantities? Which products do they need in order to produce those sales? Determine the products and volumes you could potentially sell.

- Who are your competitors? What is their position in the market?

Once you have determined those factors, and depending on the size of the account, you may decide to make joint sales calls with some of your key management staff. But remember to keep your report brief. We all know that the longer the report, the less likely it is that the people who receive it will read it. I would suggest that you keep your objective sheet to a single page per account, and be very specific. This is especially helpful when you have to keep track of a large number of accounts. The longer you maintain the sales coverage responsibility for a given account, the more advanced your objectives will become. It is good to have a copy of your manager's objectives, so that you can blend your objectives as a team and receive your manager's understanding and agreement.

It is also a good exercise to establish written objectives for each call you make; this will assure that you cover everything that needs attention. Your objectives can be as simple as a handwritten page of topics that you need to cover, and you can check each item off as you go through it during your meeting. The more calls you make on your customer, the more issues you will have to cover. The deeper you get into discussions around those issues, the more information you can find out about your customer, and the closer you become to the individuals with whom you are communicating.

No matter the size of the account, take time to review

your objectives for that visit. Who will you be visiting? What message do you want to leave with specific individuals? What subjects will you be discussing with others? What is the current year-to-date business you want to review? Are the totals by materials versus contract volumes above or below targets? Why? Are there any issues you are currently working on? Are there any disputed invoices, pricing, or billing issues that need to be addressed? These can all be sorted out through your customer service group. And last, but not least, thank the customer for the business and establish the timing for your next visit.

As my opening sentence stated, *take time to review your objectives for the call, and make sure you cover all the issues.*

Call in advance for your appointment and establish the subjects you want to discuss. Be sure to ask if there are any specific topics your customer wants to cover. This will allow your meetings to be more productive and will give you time to prepare to respond to your customer's issues with solid facts, while showing respect to your customer. It has been my experience that this helps you obtain future appointments. If your clients are always pressed for time, they will know that when you call again for an appointment, you will be organized and are not just coming in to "shoot the breeze." If you are meeting a customer that you like to entertain with a lunch date, this can be established during your telephone call. Estimate the time you'll need to discuss the topics you want to review, and allow yourself the proper amount of time. Following up with a lunch is a good touch.

As you prepare for your meeting, keep in mind the objectives you are trying to achieve with your customer. Know the questions that you want to ask. *Sell your benefits.* Understand your customer's needs and potential. Find out what it will take for your client to assign to you the share or percentage of business that you are targeting.. *Sell your benefits while asking for the order.*

At the conclusion, when you ask for future orders, be sure to *thank* your customer for the business you're receiving.

Know who the decision makers are, do not overlook them, know who the employees are in that company, be polite, and show respect to everyone. Sell yourself, your products, and the benefits that dealing with your company will give a client.

If there are several departments or groups within the organization, such as a purchasing department, a research, marketing, or manufacturing department, you should know the key personnel in all areas. Know their objectives, know how your company resources can benefit each of these areas, and use that knowledge to build credibility for yourself and your company. Use your company's internal resources, such as the staff in the research and development, distribution, engineering, marketing, and sales management departments to help you build these in-depth relationships.

This is often the start of the process when you locate a new customer that has no previous record with your company.

Know where you have been, by informing others who will have contacts with this potential customer where your company stands in the negotiating process. Therefore, all of the people involved will be on the same page. *Know where you are currently in terms of changes to* the account. For example, there may have been changes in personnel or location at the company that you are targeting. Your competitors may have changed their strategies, thus opening the door for your company to make a move. Again, advise all parties on the present activities. *Know where you are going.* You can lay out your business objectives on where you are headed. You can also outline several key issues or requirements that will impact the success of those objectives.

At the end of each quarter, you can utilize this data you've collected to communicate with your managers at the end of each quarter, giving a one-page summary of your top ten accounts.

~ Chapter 3 ~

Know Your Products

WHAT ARE THE PRODUCTS YOU are selling, and how are they produced? What does the manufacturing process entail? Are any materials that your competitors produce blended into the manufacturing process?

As a salesperson, learning everything there is to know about your product is the first step. The second step you will want to understand is your customers' needs, how your products are being used in their manufacturing process, and which competitors' materials they use.

For example, when I was involved with a soap-bar production company, the manufacturer wanted their soap bar to have a more slippery feeling. The company I worked for at the time was producing a product that could be added to the soap production formula to give that feeling. Because our R & D staff knew what the customer was trying to acquire, they produced some soap bar samples that showed very promising results. As the development proceeded, we collaborated with the technical personnel and made several further changes in our product. The results were "new" sales of 6 million dollars a year. More importantly, we developed some very solid relationships.

This demonstrates the importance of not only knowing your products, but also of collaborating with different departments within your organization and building a good relationship with your customer's research and development (R & D) group. These groups work daily to improve their products, trying to gain the edge on their competitors'.

At the same time, as the salesperson in charge of the account, always keep your purchasing group informed on what you are doing within their R&D group. Effective communications with those departments will often place you (and your company) in a very favorable position for new business.   In chapter 2, we discussed establishing objectives. The soap-bar example also demonstrates that the longer you maintain the sales coverage of specific accounts, the deeper you and your company become involved, the more opportunities you will have to understand your customer and the direction they are heading. This makes it much easier to establish objectives, while demonstrating to your management the professional leadership you are building with your accounts.   Another advantage of in-depth product knowledge becomes evident when you have developed good relations with the purchasing department at a client company. When a new sale is negotiated, try to establish a Quality Assessment (QA) Team between your company's Technical personnel and their counterparts at the client company. This allows you to sell in-depth, while establishing stronger relationships with your customer's company in departments other than the purchasing group.

Here are a few examples of the make-up of a QA Team. Note that the titles can vary:

Your Company............Customer
Salesperson.................Buyer/PA
R&D Manager..............Technical/R&D Manager
Product Manager..........Product Development Manager
Distribution Manager......Manager of Product Storage

Additionally, you will want to work jointly with the PA/ Buyer to determine the exact personnel to involve in such meetings. It will often become your responsibility to orchestrate and organize this QA team and establish the date, time, and the agenda items for meetings. This role will position you to better understand your customer, and at the same time, it places your company in a very favorable position. This process enables you to learn a great deal of information about your customers and the direction in which they are going.

Product Specifications: This is a very important process that needs to be addressed before you release a product for shipment to your customer. Fully approving the product specifications prior to shipment eliminates numerous potential problems. This becomes especially critical if you and your competitors happen to share a storage facility.

This can become a major issue during contract negotiations. If your client company has not fully approved your product specifications (preferably in writing), this can cause your bid to be eliminated from the biding process. As the salesman, this key step is your number one objective in making sure that your product specifications are fully approved before you submit your bid.

Your R&D group should have a very good understanding of the competitors' products. This is of the utmost importance, especially if your company's products are mingled with your competitors' at the customer's storage facilities. Conversely, if you don't know your competitors' products, you won't be able to distinguish issues that pertain to your products from those that pertain to the competitors'.

SCORE

UNION CARBIDE CORPORATION
Chemicals & Plastics

**Southeast Area
Refrigerant Sales Force**

O. H. CASTO, JR.

**Sales Development
Second Half 1972**

~ Chapter 4 ~

Know Your Competition

KNOWING YOUR COMPETITION IS A very important and ongoing process. Your business manager is likely to ask you several times about the competition: What are the prices and terms that Company "A", "B," or "C" have set? Which strategies do competitors have in place for sales controls?

You are your company's eyes and ears, or one might say that you are where the "rubber hits the road." If you can provide timely feedback about the competitors' activities, this information will be priceless to your management. It also gives you and your company a knowledge base that will encourage your customers to view you as the industry leader. This will often pay dividends in the form of increased business.

Here are a few topics about which you may want to gather data:

- What is the name of your competitor? Who are the principal decision-makers in that company?

- What is the competitor's main production line?

- Where are they located?

- What is their production capacity?

- What are the strengths and weakness of their raw materials?

- What is their preferred method in selling their products? For example, do they rely on direct sales or distributors?

- What has their history been comparing both methods: direct sales coverage versus distributors?

- How visible is their top management with your customers?

- In what style and manner do your competitors entertain their customers? Who do they entertain? How often do they invite their clients, and who attends those functions?

- Who is the person responsible for organizing social events that involve the clients and their company?

Analyze your competitors and their pricing policies. You must also look at the size of the market and the number of competitors who are participating in that particular market. How critical is this product to your competitor's overall business? If you were to take a large segment or volume away from their market share, what reaction could you expect? Is your competitor likely to cut the price, making the business less profitable to all?

These are some of the questions that you should consider

as you make recommendations to your manager, especially if you are recommending taking a large segment of business away from the competition. Your marketing management department can provide you with some direction in this area: your marketing manager will be aware of profit margins and understand how this fits into most of the competitors' profit line.

I have been in this exact position as a salesman, I can honestly say that I worked diligently over a period of five to six years with a major account, building relationships between key personnel at the potential customer and with several members of my management. Though I had no sales to justify this activity, I just continued focusing on the large potential. As it turned out, this particular customer announced that they were building another large plant. The plan was for the new plant to produce the same product and use the same materials as they had been using at the plant where I was spending all that time.

The end result was that my company was awarded a five-year contract, supplying 125 million pounds of product per year. Looking back on those events, I had spent a long haul without any sales to show for it over that period of time. However, the building of relationships over those five to six years paid huge *dividends.*

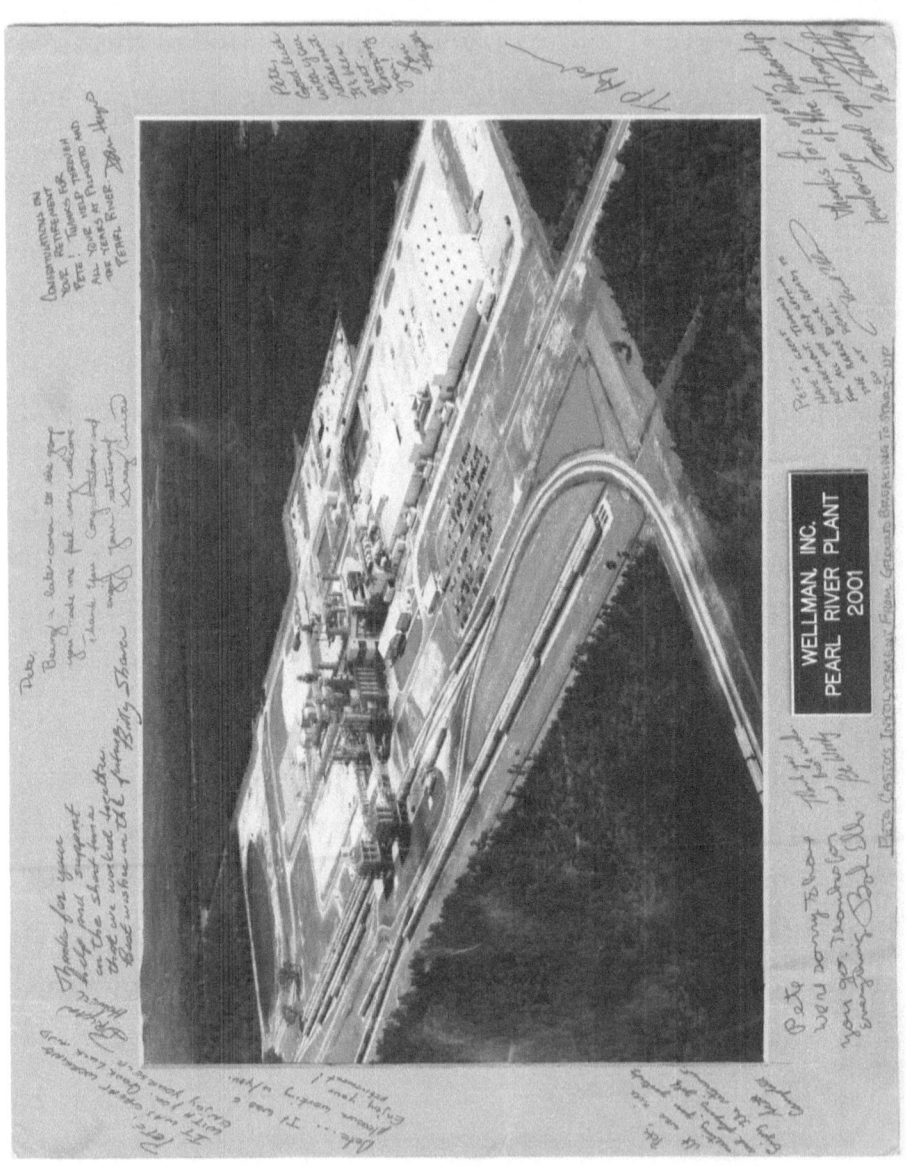

WELLMAN, INC.
PEARL RIVER PLANT
2001

~ Chapter 5 ~

Know Your Customers

KNOWING YOUR CUSTOMERS WILL REQUIRE a time investment that's proportionate to the size of your client's company, as you will need to familiarize yourself with the people in charge of the various departments that can impact your sales. Customers are your bread and butter. As in getting to know your competition, one of your initial jobs will be to gather information while getting to know your accounts. Where are they located? Who are the key decision makers? What products will you be selling? Some of these accounts may already be doing business with your company; these will be the easy ones for you to wrap your arms around. You will be able to gather data in existing files while interviewing sales and management personnel within your company; this will provide you with some very valuable information.

Another key source of information lies within the customer service department where shipping data is maintained. This takes time, and in the cases where your company has had no previous business dealings with this client, you must start from scratch to develop you own relationships. In the process, you need to communicate with the purchasing department in the client company, and you have to search for ways that may allow you to get a foot in the door to meet with the technical personnel, field storage personnel, or other upper-management staff members. This is where you began to grow as a salesperson, and you look for opportunities to establish your company and its products as a potential supplier.

As you take on a new sales territory, you may find that you need to repair damage to business relationships that any number of issues can generate. Some could have resulted from the previous salesperson offering, but not following up on certain pricing terms and conditions, causing a rift between the companies. As you assume the sales coverage of the account, you find yourself in the middle of the conflict. Depending on the complexity of the problem, it could take you some time to correct and smooth out the relationship. Every salesperson has been in this situation at some point. It is best to let the customer vent, but don't take it personally. If you don't know the facts and can rely only on what your customer is relaying, it's best to listen, and then go back to your manager to find out as much as you can about the issue. There may be good reasons as to why your company took such actions or business decisions. On your next call to your customer, when the subject comes up again, you might attempt to explain your company's position.

As you search your geographical areas for potentially new customers, you will find that most states publish manufacturing directories. These listings show the countries in which manufacturing facilities are located, what they produce, and the names of each company's top management personnel. If you attend annual conventions that are held by the businesses with which your customers are associated, you'll find that this is another possibility for locating new customers.

As an example, when I was selling products into the Air Condition and Refrigeration Industry (ACRI), the ACRI held annual conventions that customers would attend from all over the country. At those functions, I made contact with several new accounts of which my management had no prior knowledge. Who were they? Where were they located? Who were the principals? As you began to build profile sheets on your new customers, you will want to know the purchasing objectives of each buyer, so that you can find ways to relate to these objectives through your products and services. In other words, present your products in a way that will make the buyer look good, while studying the following considerations:

- To what extent are the company's employees in the purchasing department protective of their position?

- Do they encourage in-depth selling within their company?

- Do they like new ideas, or do they fear changes that may "rock the boat"? Do they merely reward new and successful ideas with lip service, or do they back up their words with additional business?

- How is new business allocated? Is it advertised so prospective supplies can place their bids? And if so, how frequently and in what manner are bids handled? Are they closed, one-shot, or best-price-winner take all type of bids?

- How are bids negotiated?

- What are the company's criteria for awarding their business? Do they make their selection based on the terms offered, pricing, or flexibility of the offer? How do they handle their pricing in the marketplace?

- How free or open are they with information? Do they keep their word? Can they be trusted with confidential information?

- What is the quality of the customer's products? Do these products have a solid position in the marketplace? Are your customers leaders in the marketplace, or are they follows? How do they penetrate the markets?

- What trade associations do they belong to? Are they leaders or attendees? Are their employees happy? Is their top management visible? Do their managers demonstrate an interest in good, solid ideas?

- How profitable is your prospective customer's company? What are their long-range goals? What is their credit rating? Is their stock traded on the NYSE or is it a closed ownership? Who are the principal owners? Are they involved partners or are they silent?

Knowing Your Customers is something that will take time. When I was assigned the sales coverage of a major market area, our company had been losing its market share annually over several years. We were the largest producer of a major product (Ethylene Glycol, Polyester Grade) used in the production of polyester fibers and polyester bottle resin known as PET. I was assigned to cover the southeastern and southwestern regions of the United States, and my goal was to rebuild our image and market share in those major areas.

It was a huge challenge, primarily because I was facing some major negative issues. I conducted many discussions with my management and a couple salespeople, who were very familiar with the issues, to gather as much information as possible. I was facing a real, uphill battle. However, this is when I put my motto into practice: "Know thy customers and know them well," and I began applying the principles of this book: *Mastering The Basics of Selling*.

To use an old cliché, I spent the next five years "walking the walk while talking the talk." In other words, I called on several of these customers on a monthly basis, selling our products' benefits, and waiting for the current contracts that my prospects held with other companies to expire. At the same time, I moved toward re-qualifying our product specifications. After about five years of persistent work to resolve these problems, I began to see positive results. The following article, published by *The Beacon* in our company, will give you details of the success that knowing your customers can bring.

SCORE

UNION
CARBIDE
CORPORATION
Chemicals & Plastics

U.S. Area
Refrigerant Sales Force

O. H. CASTO, JR.

Outstanding Salesmanship
First Half 1971

Customer Focus:

The Road to Success for EOG's Pete Casto

Know thy customers – and know them well. Undoubtedly this is the credo of EOG's Pete Casto who, with dogged determination and sheer persistence, pursued several potential customers

Pete Casto pursues customers with persistence and vigor.

for five years, waiting for an opportunity to serve them. "Pete was so successful in this endeavor," says Bob Nelson, former EOG business director and current president of EQUATE Marketing Company, "that in 1995, we negotiated contracts that will double our U.S. polyester glycol business by 1999. And for his efforts, Pete won a Chairman's Award."

For 15 years, Carbide's polyester glycol market share in North America had been steadily declining. A key strategic initiative for EOG was to gain supply positions at several target domestic accounts. Pete heeded this

call to action. With support from all across Carbide, he spent five years patiently cultivating a relationship with ICI and other major accounts. He called on them regularly – even when past attempts to secure their business had failed.

Despite his frustration, Pete was determined to keep Carbide in the forefront. He actively pursued these accounts, biding his time until new opportunities arose. He kept abreast of their new plant start-ups as well as their need for additional supply sources. When the time was right, Carbide would be ready, willing and able to become their preferred new supplier.

In 1995, a year of unprecedented opportunity in the domestic polyester glycol market, Pete capitalized on some unique opportunities. Current supplier contracts were expiring, new polyester plants were starting up, and additional glycol supply sources were needed. Pete was first in their doors. He targeted his proposals to meet each customer's needs. He resolved their concerns, bulldogged the process, and ultimately succeeded in negotiating several multi-year contracts.

By bringing value to customers, by focusing on results that support Carbide's strategy, and by promoting teamwork, Pete Casto accomplished a triple win—for the customers, for Carbide and for himself.

Lee McMaster

1995 Chairman's Awards

The successes of our 1995 Chairman's Award teams have brought many benefits to EOG, and for those we thank all the winners. We especially thank Pete Casto, whose customer-focused efforts vastly improved our domestic supply position. You can read more about Pete's accomplishments on page 4. In addition, Geza Azsoth, Doug Canfield, Kathy George, Lester Haydel, Gus McLaren and Jeff Pauley deserve special mention for their superb work on the Higher Glycols Operations Team. Their efforts will be highlighted in our next issue.

~ Chapter 6 ~

Don't Make Promise You Can't Keep

PROTECTING ONE'S CREDIBILITY AS A salesperson is the most important thing a salesperson can do. Your credibility will follow you throughout your career. There will be times when you confront opportunities and are tempted to make a promise that could land you a large piece of business. However, if you were to find out later that your business manager will not support that promise, this would place you in an embarrassing position.

If and when that should ever develop, it would take that particular customer some time to gain trust in you again. The failed promise may have encouraged your customer to go back to the second supplier (who had, at first, been unsuccessful at competing with you) and ask that supplier to reinstate his bid. The supplier may or may not offer the original pricing and terms. This could put you in a no win position over a long period of time.

This is why it is very important that the buyer give you a written document that clearly states the product, its specifications, and the volume for which you are bidding, along with the shipments modes, where shipments are to be made, and the duration of the agreement.

At the same time, it is best that your business group

communicate their support for this business. This document becomes a good track record for any future sales person who may assume responsibility for the account in the event that you move to another position.

Another area where confusion can exist is when a competitor comes in after you have been awarded the business, by offering an off-spec product at a lower price and terms. The buyer may then present this offer to you, and ask that you either meet those terms or release the buyer from the contract. This is likely to happen at some point in a salesperson's career. Therefore, it's important to have the contract incorporate specifications of the product you will be shipping. You can then request the buyer to provide you with a copy of the competitor's specification, or a sample of the product they are offering at the lower price.

Building your product specifications into the proposal itself gives you a solid position to defend your bid or proposal. You can then let the competitor take the business, or your company may likewise have off-spec materials that could match the competitor's price, thereby allowing you to keep the business.

~ *Chapter 7* ~

Maintain Timely Communication

THE INFORMATION THAT YOU COMMUNICATE to your management on your top twelve customers should include some of the history on where you have been, where you are, and your objectives on where you are planning to go with each customer. This keeps everyone in the management chain fully informed. They will have clear understanding of the total picture and make sure that the staff in your management and marketing departments understand and fully support your policies. It's your road map; keep it up to date.

Utilize your time in a most productive manner when communicating. Use the telephone, electronic mail service, voice mailbox system, text messaging, etc., as required. If you are using the telephone and were not able to reach your party, always leave a brief message regarding the topic or subject matter you wanted to discuss. This enables your party to be prepared when you call back. It is also nice to e-mail an advance copy of your agenda for up-coming appointments, to make your meetings more productive.

When you communicate a request to your management, or when you offer a proposal to a customer, be sure to lay out your recommendations and project what you think the results may be, never promising more than you can deliver. If you don't know the answer or feel that you are going out too far on a limb, say so. Knowing your organization will help you in these areas. Management generally monitors key accounts and large volume-type accounts. When you know that your management is keeping an eye on the progress, you will want to communicate any problems and opportunities in a timely manner. Always obtain as much information as possible, and be ready for your manager to call you, seeking as much information as you may have. When you outline a problem, do so to the best of your knowledge and recommend solutions. You are more than likely the closest to the situation. Always look at each problem as an opportunity; never "push it under the rug, hoping that it will to go away." The approach will most likely move you and your business right out the door.

~ Chapter 8 ~

Start Your Sales Career

So, HERE YOU ARE. YOU have been given an opportunity and assigned a territory to develop sales. This may be an existing sales region with existing sales data, or a new area altogether. You will want to quickly make an impact and gain recognition. Where do you start?

First, let's take a look at your current top ten or fifteen accounts on record. Utilize the planning sheets shown in the Appendix section. Using this format, you can build a tremendous picture of the account. Compile the known data, pick the brains of your management, customer service personnel, and former salespeople (if available) who would be familiar with the region. Since you are just getting started, compile as much data as you can.

After you get your hands and brain wrapped around this task, arrange a meeting with your first customer to introduce yourself to the key contacts within that company. This meeting, being your first contact, can allow you to make a good first impression.

It also will allow you to gain an impression of how the buyer feels about your company. Your first meeting allows you to ask questions toward establishing ground rules that this buyer or purchasing agent will want to follow as you move forward. The purpose of this initial meeting is to collect data;

when you set up your initial call, try to schedule enough time so that you can get most of your questions answered.

Once you have established face-to-face contact, you can follow up with telephone calls, again filling in more data on your account profile. Now you're on your way to getting a meeting established with your manager. Allow enough time to discuss your top accounts. This meeting will allow you to review the data on record, and, more importantly, it starts the process of developing and establishing the framework of your business objectives, strategies, and timing with your manager. This is a key process and as your knowledge increases, you may want to revisit these objectives.

This process allows you to look at each account to determine the following factors:

- Where you and your company have been with this customer

- Where your company is positioned currently

- Where you are planning on taking your company

As you begin putting together these profiles, you'll become more knowledgeable and confident. As a result, you'll be able to give your management team a better understanding of what your customers are planning.. You are building internal knowledge that will pay dividends. Yes, this is a lot of data that will need continual updating, but selling in-depth will protect your business and go a long way toward improving sales. And the ensuing results will not come as a surprise. As personnel move from one position to another, your in-depth knowledge will aid you in building sales dollars and volume.

~ *Chapter 9* ~

Something to Think About

FALLING INTO A RUT CAN happen to any of us! Let's look at a scenario that illustrates the *Back to Basics concept:*

I would imagine that most salespeople today have an interest in sports of some form, and that they read published sports-related articles. I'm a baseball fan, and when a baseball team is experiencing a long losing streak, the manager often says: "We're going back to the basics." This is, likewise, true in several other sports. Prime examples are articles on "Back to Basics" often written in various magazines, where golf professionals explain how to get your game in shape fast. The finest golf professionals today all recognize the value of going back to basics.

Well, salespeople are not much different than professional athletes or organized sports teams. We work in a very competitive atmosphere constantly. Only the names of the activities are different. We often become so familiar with our job that we tend to look for shortcuts, or we just take our job for granted. By going back to the basics, we can change old habits and fine-tune our selling skills to increase sales accomplishments.

During the past twenty-five years, it's been my observation and experience that staying with the "basics" of selling has brought forth more positive results than any other gimmick

I could have tried. This approach has enabled me to earn several outstanding salesmanship awards, along with several promotions.

In my personal life, I have had the great pleasure of seeing my annual sales in each of my last fifteen years surpass the sales of the preceding year. I attribute my successes at obtaining these records to my ability to maintaining a close focus on *The Basics of Selling.*

~ Chapter 10 ~

Letters of My Promotions and Awards

THROUGHOUT MY CAREER IN SALES, as I "talked the talk and walked the walk," I stayed the course, just as I have outlined in *Mastering the Basics of Selling*. The results have earned me several promotions and awards. The more successful I became, the more my sales volume increased, the more dollars I earned annually.

This chapter includes several of my promotion letters to prove my point. Several of my sales awards are also positioned throughout my book.

UNION CARBIDE CORPORATION

CHEMICALS AND PLASTICS

26500 NORTHWESTERN HIGHWAY, SOUTHFIELD, MICHIGAN 48076

June 3, 1974

To all Chemicals and Plastics
    Sales and Marketing Personnel

    We are pleased to announce the promotion of O. H. Casto, Jr. to Area Sales Manager with the General Sales Force. Pete will headquarter in Southfield, Michigan, and have Field Sales responsibility for Market Areas 122, 123, 124, 125.

    Pete's Continuous Service Date is December 1957 at which time he initiated his career with Union Carbide at South Charleston as a draftsman. He grew to Senior draftsman, Product Group Assistant, and then to Engineering Assistant. In 1969 he moved to Atlanta, Georgia, as a Technical Representative and was promoted to Area Representative in 1970.

    Pete has long been recognized as having developed into a top flight professional salesman and in fact, for the first half of 1972, after spending a relatively short time in the Sales Department was given the Outstanding Salesman's Award.

    We congratulate Pete on his new assignment and look forward to his continued growth.

George E. Kuehn
Director of Sales

William P. Emerson
National Sales Manager

UNION CARBIDE CORPORATION

CHEMICALS AND PLASTICS

270 PARK AVENUE, NEW YOR, N.Y. 10017

CONTACT: Nancy M. Bischoff   FOR RELEASE: Immediately
         (212) 551-2129

Union Carbide Names Orville H. Casto, Jr.
               District Sales Manager
_____

New York, NY -- Orville H. (Pete) Casto, Jr. has been promoted
to District Sales Manager in the Industrial & Specialty Chemicals Sales
Force, Union Carbide Corporation.

Mr. Casto graduated from West Virginia State College,
Institute, WV, with a BA in Mathematics. He joined Union Carbide in 1957
as a draftsman trainee in South Charleston, WV, and spent the next
twelve years as Senior Draftsman & Engineering Assistant.

His first sales assignment was as a Technical Representative in
Refrigerant Sales in Atlanta, and he was subsequently promoted to Area
Sales Manager in Industrial & Specialty Sales, in Detroit. As District
Sales Manager, he will remain in Detroit.

Mr. Casto is a native of Clendenin, WV, and is married to the
former Judy Marks. The Castos live in Rochester, MI.

# # # #

January 9, 1979

UNION CARBIDE CORPORATION 39 OLD RIDGEBURY ROAD, DANBURY, CT 06817-0001

W. H. JOYCE
CHAIRMAN AND
CHIEF EXECUTIVE OFFICER

March 15, 1995

Mr. O.H. Casto, Jr.
3017 Poplar Hill Rd.
Charlotte, NC 28270

Dear Pete:

Congratulations on being named a 1995 Chairman's Award winner. You can take great pride in being among those chosen from an outstanding group of nominees around the world.

Carbide's success in 1995 resulted from tireless efforts by employees to continuously improve the efficiency and safety of our operations, control costs, and serve our customers. Our Chairman's Award winners led these efforts. Whatever the challenge, you aimed high, persevered despite setbacks and exceeded expectations. Your exceptional performance serves as a model for others.

I look forward to celebrating this well-deserved honor with you and your associates and guests during a special Chairman's Award Day. Your local management will provide the details and answer any questions.

My heartiest congratulations and appreciation for your commitment to our company's values, goals and winning behaviors. Efforts such as yours help ensure that Union Carbide will continue to prosper and grow. I look forward to personally presenting your award and thanking you for your contribution to Carbide's success.

Sincerely,

Bill

WHJ/ddg

64

65

UNION CARBIDE CORPORATION
Industrial Chemicals Division

39 Old Ridgebury Road
Danbury, CT 06817-0001

TO: All ICD employees

DATE: April 16, 1986

It is a pleasure to announce the appointment of O. H. Casto to the position of Account Executive in Charlotte, NC. Pete will be taking over from Walt Locher who is retiring on June 30.

Pete Casto, who is a real Carbide native from the birthplace of petrochemicals, Clendenin, West Virginia, started his career at our Charleston works in 1956 and has distinguished himself in various sales assignments. His most recent hitch has been District Sales Manager of our Western Region in Long Beach, California.

Replacing Walt Locher, who is our foremost authority on the polyester resin industry and best understands the needs of this special group of ICD customers for our ethylene glycol, will not be easily accomplished. Walt's thirty seven plus years of experience are evident in the warm and effective relationships he has established with his key accounts - Eastman, Celanese, American Hoechst, Firestone, and Akzona.

Walt will be sorely missed but Pete will be an effective successor at this key sales responsibility for ICD and Union Carbide. Best of luck to you Walt in your well deserved retirement and also great success to Pete in your continuing Carbide career.

Pete Casto will report to Al Donaldson in our Atlanta regional office.

1075M

H. E. Klein

Pete - You will do well in your new assignment! As a matter of fact you will most probably be setting the "standard" for the rest of us! Regards, your friend Rich

~ Appendix ~

Proposed Account Format Planning Sheets

TAKE TIME TO ASSEMBLE FOR yourself a complete "who's who" informational directory. You will find that many times, a document that contains all the contact information will come in handy and save you countless hours.

Information of this type is particularly useful when you are arranging for joint calls with other personnel within your company, or when you are called upon in your annual review of customers.

Company Names _____

Address _____

Telephone # _____

Fax# _____

E-mail _____

Key Contacts

CEO _____

Phone # _____

Activities/Interests _____

President _____

Phone # _____

Activities/Interests _____

Director of Purchasing _____

Phone # _____

Activities/Interests _____

Key Buyer (A) _____

Products _____

Phone # _____

Activities/Interests _____

Key Buyer (B) _____

Products _____

Phone #_____

Activities/Interests _____

Key Buyer (C) _____

Products _____

Phone # _____

Activities/Interests _____

Key Buyer (D) _____

Products _____

Phone # _____

Activities/Interests _____

<u>Key Warehouse/Receiving Names/Titles</u>

Name _____

Title _____

Phone # _____

Fax# _____

Activities/Interests _____

Key Credit Management
Name _____
Title _____
Phone # _____
E-mail _____
Activities/Interests _____

R&D/Technical Personnel

Name _____
Product Area _____
Phone # _____
Fax# _____
E-mail Address _____

Travel/Directions from Airport

_____
_____
_____
_____
_____
_____

Your Company's Sales Records by Products/lbs

Products by Name Listed Below and Pounds Sold/Yr.	2009	2010	2011	Total lbs. Potential

Competitors & Sales by Pounds/Yr.	%Share			

Your Company

Strengths: _____

_____

Weaknesses: _____

_____

Competition

Strengths: _____

_____

Weaknesses: _____

_____

Company (A):

Know Where You Have Been: _____

_____

_____

_____

_____

Know Where You Are Currently: _____

_____

_____

_____

_____

Know Where You Are Going (Be sure your management is on board):

_____

_____

_____

_____

Company (B):

Know Where You Have Been: _____

_____

_____

_____

_____

Know Where You Are Currently: _____

_____

_____

_____

_____

Know Where You Are Going (Be sure your management is on board):

_____

_____

_____

_____

Company (C):

Know Where You Have Been: _____

_____

_____

_____

_____

Know Where You Are Currently: _____

_____

_____

_____

_____

Know Where You Are Going (Be sure your management is on board):

_____

_____

_____

_____

Company (D):

Know Where You Have Been: _____

_____

_____

_____

_____

Know Where You Are Currently: _____

_____

_____

_____

Know Where You Are Going (Be sure your management is on board):

_____

_____

_____

_____

Preparing Yourself for Each Sales Call

\>Objective? _____

\>Who you will meet? _____

_____

_____

\>Timing? Names? Lunch? Dinner? _____

_____

_____

\>Key Points to be Made at Each Event? _____

_____

_____

\>Take Good Notes _____

_____

_____

_____

_____

_____

>Establish next meeting _____
Date/Time and any required action promised the customer
with timing to get back with answers _____

_____

_____

_____

_____

Key Internal Personnel- Communication

Name _____

E-mail _____

Name _____

E-mail _____

Name _____

E-mail _____

Name _____

E-mail _____

Name _____

E-mail _____

Name _____

E-mail _____

Name _____

E-mail _____

Name _____

E-mail _____

The following are key pieces of information that should be covered in Report of Calls

_____

_____

_____

_____

_____

_____

>Major Problems / Major Accomplishments

>Major Competitors' Moves

>Credit Issues

>Quarterly Summaries / Year-End Summaries

>Keep them brief, addressing the key points and where you are versus your objective and any required action steps

>Recommendations that you feel as the Saleperson will solve existing problem areas and or successfully achieve the outlined objectives.

www.ingramcontent.com/pod-product-compliance
Lightning Source LLC
Chambersburg PA
CBHW022104170526
45157CB00004B/1474